Everything Flows
A Celebration of the Transporter Bridge in Poetry
edited by Andy Croft

First published in Great Britain by Middlesbrough Borough Council, 2012

No part of this book may be reproduced or transmitted in any form or by any means without written permission from the publisher, except by a reviewer who wishes to quote a brief passages in connection with a review written for insertion in a magazine, newspaper, internet website or broadcast.

copyright 2012, the authors

Cover painting: Alan Morley, *Impression, Sunrise over the Tees* (Oil on Board, 2008)

ISBN 0-86083-092-6

Hail Teesside!

Old ironmasters and their iron men
With northern fire, grit, enterprise began it
A hundred years ago. Later, we scan it –
Desolate homesteads welded into one,
Hamlets grown up to towns, deep anchorage
Gouged out of sand, wastes blossoming with the fierce
White rose of foundries. So the pioneers
Printed their work on nature's open page.
Their steel made bridges from Sydney to Menai ;
Their shops networked the sea. Gain was in view
But inch by inch out of the gain there grew
A greater thing – a sense of community.

Bridges are for drawing men together
By closing gaps. Could those rough ghosts return,
They'd find a world of difference, but discern
That here is the same breed of men and weather.
You are bridge builders still. Only today
You draw six towns into a visioned O,
Spanning from town to town the ebb and flow
Of destiny. A dream is realised. May
The northern kindliness and northern pride
See, as your forebears would, the future in it.
Here a new span – our lives shall underpin it
And earn fresh honours for our own Teesside.

Cecil Day Lewis

When the new County Borough of Teesside was set up in 1968, the Evening Gazette asked Cecil Day Lewis, then Poet Laureate, to write a poem to celebrate the occasion.

'Hail Teesside!' appears here by permission of the literary estate of Cecil Day Lewis.

Introduction

'Earth has not anything to show more fair:
Dull would be he of soul who could pass by
A sight so touching in its majesty'
William Wordsworth, 'Upon Westminster Bridge'

Everyone likes a good bridge. There is something strange and magical about the way that bridges combine the elements, connecting earth by air over water. Every bridge is a crossing place and a meeting place, a point of arrival and departure. It's a short-cut from here to there, a transport solution and a stunning feat of engineering. The longest bridge in the world, the Danyang-Kunshan railway bridge in China, is 165,000 metres long. One of the oldest surviving bridges in the world, built in Greece in the 13th century BC, is still in daily use.

You can pass over a bridge or you can pass under it. When you are on a bridge you are in no-man's land. Bridges are sites of disasters and accidents and suicides. In ancient myths, bridges often led from this world to the land of the dead. A bridge is a piece of history and a working museum. It's a piece of public art, something to look at and a place from which to look at the world. Bridges bring people together. We warn people not to burn their bridges. We like those who build bridges.

The Transporter Bridge, linking the Middlesbrough and Stockton banks of the River Tees, is one of the North-east's most iconic landmarks. The longest surviving Transporter Bridge in the world (there were once twenty bridges of this type), the Tranny is 260 metres long and 70 metres tall, and swings traffic over the river on a gondola. It is a working bridge, an engineering miracle, a work of art and a monument to Teesside's industrial history.

All the best bridges have their place in literary history – notably the Tay Bridge (William McGonagall) the Forth Bridge (Iain Banks) and Waterloo Bridge (Thomas Hood). Brooklyn Bridge in New York has inspired by many distinguished writers, including Walt Whitman, Jack Kerouac, Hart Crane and Arthur Miller.

The Transporter Bridge is no exception. It has been celebrated in song by Graeme Miles and Erik Gooding; and featured in novels by Margaret Drabble, Pat Barker, Freya North and Stephen Baker. It has been widely featured on film and TV, from *Boys from the Blackstuff* and *Billy Elliot* to *Auf Wiedersehen Pet*.

This book of poems is a contribution to the celebrations marking the bridge's centenary. I guessed that there would be some interest locally in the idea of a book of poems about the Transporter, but the scale and the speed of the response took me completely by surprise. A couple of quick appeals in the *Evening Gazette*, the *Northern Echo* and on BBC Radio Tees, and the poems started to arrive. They came in from Middlesbrough, Port Clarence, Stockton, Redcar and Hartlepool, from Guisborough and Stokesley, from Wearside and Tyneside. There is even one poem here sent in by a Teesside exile working in Dubai.

There were poems from primary schools, secondary schools, holiday clubs and local history reminiscence groups. Some were written especially for this book; some are by previously published poets, most are not. For reasons of budget and space I have not been able to include every poem in this book, but I have tried, as far as possible, to represent the range and the richness of the many poems I received.

Westminster Bridge is older, the Humber Bridge is longer and the Tyne Bridge is better-known. But it is hard to think of another bridge in the UK that generates so much affection as the Transporter does. Or any bridge that could inspire so many poems. And yet this is not a book of poems about a bridge. It is a book about belonging, about class and work and history, about ideas of community and feelings of identity. These are essentially love poems to Teesside, past and present, real and imagined.

Andy Croft, Middlesbrough 2012

The Tees Transporter Bridge, one of the few remaining operational transporter bridges worldwide, has been a symbol of the area since it opened in 1911. Serving as an important crossing point between Middlesbrough and Port Clarence, this world-renowned structure rises from the banks of the River Tees to dominate the Teesside skyline. As the Transporter enters a new chapter in its life, it continues to stand proudly both as an enduring and defiant legacy of the area's industrial heritage and as an icon of progress and development.

Tosh Warwick
Transporter Bridge Education, Learning and Events Officer
Middlesbrough Council

Contents

13	Sloppy Molly	Kathleen Larkin
13	A Real Beauty	Port Clarence group
15	Clarence Kids, 100 Years Ago	Tamzin Hunter, Kennedy Hutchinson and Courtney McWilliams
15	What's the Transporter, Like?	Lee Kerridge
16	Why is the Transporter Blue?	Courtney Kelly, Kiera Kelly and Natasha Witham
16	Sunshine or Fog	David Fenwick
17	Heritage	Easterside Library Group
17	Birthday Memories	Ormesby Library group
19	What is a Bridge?	Easterside Library Group
20	How the Bridge Became	Trinity Community Centre, North Ormesby
23	Transporter Bridge	David Walland
25	It's a Boy!	Ormesby Library group
25	Good Question	Roy G Robertson
25	She	Ian Yarrow
26	Everything Flows	Ormesby Library group
28	What Does the Bridge Remember?	Easterside Library Group
28	A Giant	Mr J Horner
29	Just the Job	South Bank Library group
30	Transported	Chris Robinson
32	Blue Dragon	David Christopher Lacey
33	Bicycle Men of the Transporter	Ian Horn
34	The Transporter	Bob Beagrie
37	Border Crossing	Andy Willoughby
38	The Transporter	Robert Instone
38	Blue Dog	Gary Smith
40	Metal Colossus in Blue	Irene Styles
41	Transported	Marilyn Longstaff
43	The Transporter	Alan E Watkiss
44	Home Run	Monica Sharp
45	M for Middlesbrough	Brian Morton
46	Ode to the Transporter	Norma Guy
47	Branded	Helen Victoria Anderson
47	The Brollys of Boro	Marilyn Longstaff
49	Transporter	Michael Brown
49	Our Transporter	Gary Wake

50	Sanctuary	Gordon Hodgeon
50	Transport us for a Century....	Karen Raby
51	Her Heart May Beat of Iron	Peter de Dee
52	Not Just a Physical Structure	Robert Alan Cowley
53	Across the Bridge to the Seaside	Garry Morrison
53	Limerick	Pat Avent
54	The Lady of the Tees	Garry Hassell
54	Cerulean	Keith Sell
55	Stronger Together	Harry Gallagher
55	The Scream	Ben Hodgson
57	The Transporter Bridge	Robert Lonsdale
58	Bridge Haikus	Boro Buzz
58	Recipe for a Bridge	Boro Buzz
59	On the Money	Ann Graal
61	Our Day in the Sun	Sean Barnes
61	Transporter	K Stephenson
62	A Hundred Years Ago	RG Phillips
62	The School Run	Liz Geraghty
63	Big Blue and Strong	Paul Adamson
63	I Stand Proud	Janet Jeffrey
65	Unbecoming	Liz Geraghty
65	Transporter Bridge	Gina Brennan
66	Transporter	Khadim Hussain
67	The Transporter	Ted Hardwick
68	A Century in Blue	Fred Jones
69	The Transporter Bridge	Alan Brownbridge
69	On a Visit to the Transporter Bridge	Jane Dunn
70	Transporter	Keith Porritt
70	Immense Changes	Mrs G Bennison
72	The Transporter Bridge	Kayla McBride
72	I Stand	Kathryn Mellor
73	Down the Ferry Road	Colleen Batey
74	Beloved Tranny	Keith Kirkbride
74	The Blue Lady of the Tees	Mick Crosby
75	Megga-Meccano	Anthony Gibson
75	Alone	Elinor Northey
76	Notice	Phil Holt-Swain
76	Glittering Gorgeously	Ellie Stephenson
77	Twin Towers	Peter Nolan
78	Bungee Jumping off the Transporter	Overfields Primary School

81	Our True Centurion	Joan Clark
81	Majestic	Martin Fletcher
82	The Sense of a Bridge	Sam Power
82	The Transporter Bridge	Luke Williams
83	The Big Blue Bridge	A Way Out/ARC
84	The River Grave	Pennyman Primary School
85	Holding On	Janet Lancefield
87	Transporter Bridge	Victoria Dolan
87	The Opening of the Transporter	Brambles Farm Primary School
88	Moving Backwards	Andy Croft
92	La Dolce Vita	Author unknown
93	My Centenary	Author unknown

Illustrations

14	Dennis Roddam	*Untitled*
18	Gillian Spensley	*Sky*
24	Charles Twist	*100 Beats of the Clock*
27	Jean Botwright	*Transporter Bridge*
31	Jean Botwright	*Lighting the Way*
36	Margery Shotton	*Transporter Gate*
39	Gillian Bradley	*Bridge #1*
42	Gillian Bradley	*Bridge #2*
48	Gillian Spensley	*The North East's Greatest*
56	Adrian Moule	*Transporter Bridge*
60	Mary Hicks	*Crossing to the Works*
64	Alan Morley	*La Middlesbrough Dance*
71	Dee Maloney	*Blue Sky over the Transporter Bridge*
80	Alan Morley	*The River Tees at Middlesbrough, 1911*
86	Dennis Roddam	*Transporter Triptych*

Sloppy Molly

Of course, we weren't supposed to.
It was dangerous.
'Don't you dare!' our Mams used to say.
They would have killed us if they knew.
But every Saturday morning
We would go down to the Tranny
To play Sloppy Molly.
The river bank was a jungle
Of gooseberry trees.
Me and Jeanie and Stephanie,
Brendan, Jimmy, Peter
And both Janets,
We crawled through the bushes,
And there in the grey mud
Beneath the legs of the bridge
At the wide river's edge,
We played at Mams and Dads,
Sloppy Molly,
Baking mud-pies with little sticks.
Then we would run back home
For our dinner,
Washing the mud off our hands
Before we were caught.

Kathleen Larkin

A Real Beauty

She's a fine old lady,
A tough old bird.
She's getting on a bit,
But still in her prime.
She's like a grandma
To all of us.

Port Clarence group

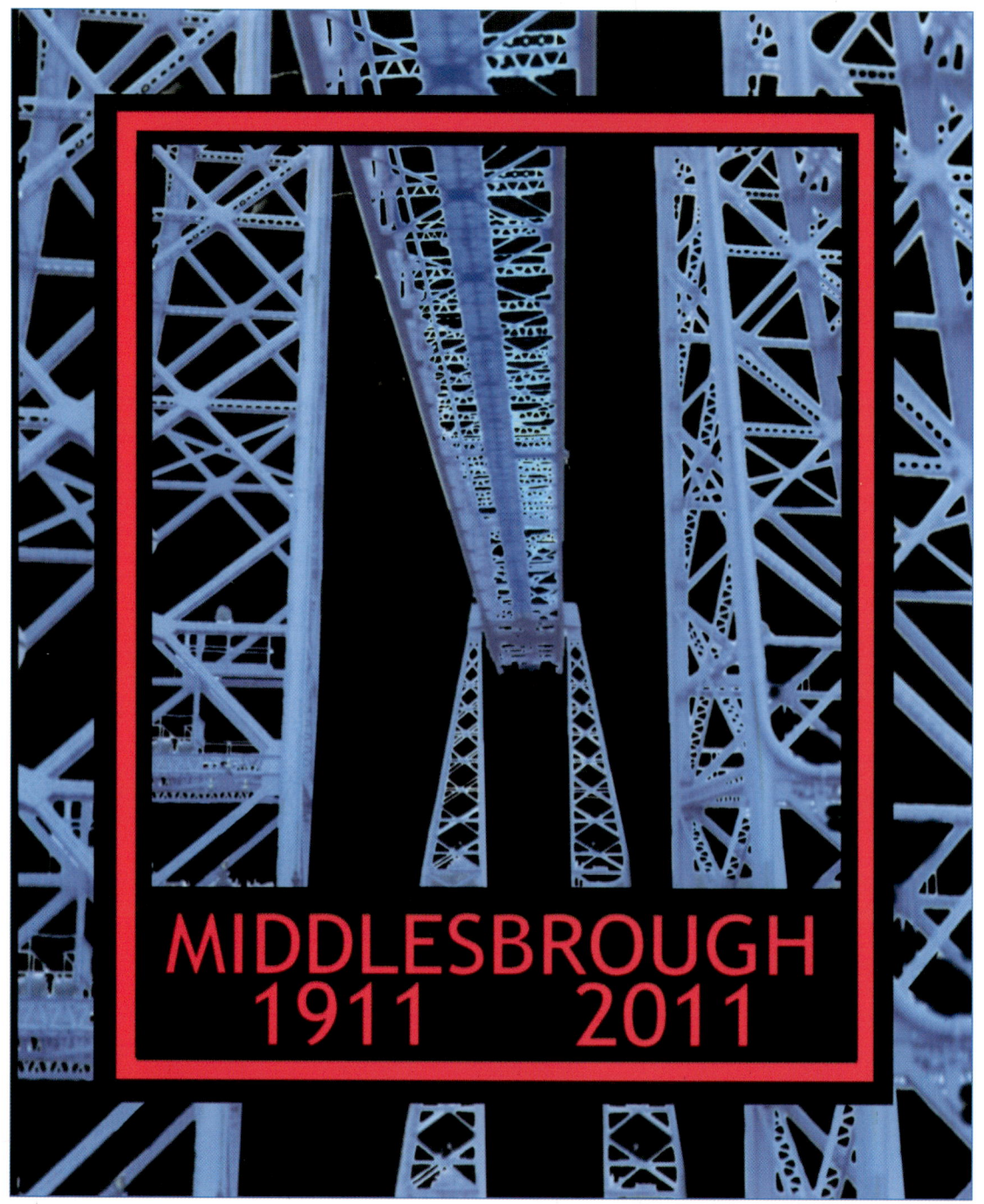

Dennis Roddam *Untitled* (Medium Unknown)

Clarence Kids, 100 Years Ago

There aren't any cars
And we can't watch tv,
We don't play on computers
Or chat on mobile-phones,
There's no hot running water
And the toilet's outside –

But we can play on the street,
Hopscotch, football, skipping games.

And we have
A big, blue, tall, metal, solid,
Scary, extreme, amazing, breath-taking
Bridge!

Tamzin Hunter, Kennedy Hutchinson and Courtney McWilliams

What's the Transporter, Like?

It has long thin legs like a giraffe,
It is busy as a big blue people carrier,
Old as our school,
Cool as ice-cream.
If the Transporter was a book,
It would be an encyclopaedia,
Full of information and facts about local history;
If the Bridge was a cake,
It would have 100 birthday candles!

Lee Kerridge

Why is the Transporter Blue?

Because if it was red,
It would look angry and out of place.
Because if it was yellow,
It would be too bright.
Because if it was silver,
It would be too sparkly.
Because if it was white,
It would look dull and dirty.
Because if it was orange,
It would look rusty.
Because if it was gold,
It would be too dazzling.
Because if it was pink,
It would be too girly.

Because a bridge of blue
Reflects the river below,
It mirrors the sky above,
And shadows the night.

And because we can't imagine
The Transporter Bridge
Being any colour
Except this
Beautiful, calm, laid-back,
Relaxed, cheerful kind of blue.

Courtney Kelly, Kiera Kelly and Natasha Witham

Sunshine or Fog

Whether sunshine or fog
The bridge can't be seen for the smog.
No wildlife no trees
Just the polluted river Tees.

David Fenwick

Heritage

It's an historic icon,
A museum piece,
A working model,
It's a brand, a logo,
It's a picture-postcard,
A souvenir for Sunday tourists,
A mecca for bungee-jumpers,
A dinosaur gathering dust and rust,
It's a memory,
An interactive exhibit,
A monument to skill, hard work, ingenuity,
sweat, labour, struggle and defeat.
It's ours.

Easterside Library Group

Birthday Memories

To celebrate the hundredth birthday of the Transporter
We would give the old bridge:
A new gondola,
An 'M' bus ticket,
A mobile made of bits from the Sidney Harbour Bridge,
A straw bonnet and a new pair of white sandals and socks,
A man's bike with a child's saddle and stirrups on the cross-bar,
A garden-swing,
A 1911 lucifer-match,
Some fairy lights,
And a great big block of Teesside steel.

Ormesby Library group

Gillian Spensley, *Sky* (Acrylic on Canvas)

What is a Bridge?

It's a crossing between places,
A connection between spaces,
A road through the air,
A step into the void.
It overcomes barriers,
Fords rivers,
Spans shores,
Fills gaps
And unites those who are divided.
It expands horizons
And raises expectations,
A link between two sides of the same earth.
It arches its back like a caterpillar,
Swings like a tarzee,
Leaps across water like a fish,
Extends like a ladder,
Reaches like a handshake.
You can trust a bridge to get you there.
It's an entrance and an exit,
A stairway to heaven,
An intrusion into the ether.
It smells of toil
And tastes of oil,
Shivering in the wind,
Groaning, straining against the weight,
It braces itself,
Grits its teeth,
Riveted to the spot.

Easterside Library Group

How the Bridge Became

This is the story of the Transporter Bridge. It begins two thousand years ago on the banks of the river Tees. There were no roads or houses then. No schools or shops. Just fields and trees. Everything was quiet. And then the Romans arrived:

Why have we stopped?
Because of the river.
Well. Let's cross it.
But how? The river's too wide.
Well, let's find a boat.
But where can we find a boat?
There's a boat over there.
But it's on the other side of the river...

Song:
Oh oh! Oh oh!
We can't get across to the other side.
Oh oh! Oh oh!
There's a very strong tide and the river's too wide.
Oh oh! Oh oh! Oh oh!

So the Romans turned round and marched away. And at the bottom of the river the trolls laughed:
No-one will ever cross this river! Ha! Ha! Ha!

Many years passed on the banks of the river. Everything was quiet. And then the Vikings arrived:

Why have we stopped?
Because of the river.
Well. Let's cross it.
But how? The river's too wide.
Well, let's find a boat.
But where can we find a boat?
There's a boat over there.
But it's on the other side of the river...

Oh oh! Oh oh!
We can't get across to the other side.
Oh oh! Oh oh!
There's a very strong tide and the river's too wide.
Oh oh! Oh oh! Oh oh!

So the Vikings turned round and marched away. And at the bottom of the river the trolls laughed: No-one will ever cross this river! Ha! Ha! Ha!

Many years passed on the banks of the river. Everything was quiet. And then the Normans arrived:

Why have we stopped?
Because of the river.
Well. Let's cross it.
But how? The river's too wide.
Well, let's find a boat.
But where can we find a boat?
There's a boat over there.
But it's on the other side of the river...

Oh oh! Oh oh!
We can't get across to the other side.
Oh oh! Oh oh!
There's a very strong tide and the river's too wide.
Oh oh! Oh oh! Oh oh!

So the Normans turned round and marched away. And at the bottom of the river the trolls laughed: No-one will ever cross this river! Ha! Ha! Ha!

Many years passed on the banks of the river. Everything was quiet. And then the monks arrived:

Why have we stopped?
Because of the river.
Well. Let's cross it.
But how? The river's too wide.
Well, let's find a boat.
But where can we find a boat?
There's a boat over there.
But it's on the other side of the river...

Oh oh! Oh oh!
We can't get across to the other side.
Oh oh! Oh oh!
There's a very strong tide and the river's too wide.
Oh oh! Oh oh! Oh oh!

So the monks turned round and marched away. And at the bottom of the river the trolls laughed: No-one will ever cross this river! Ha! Ha! Ha!

Many years passed on the banks of the river. Everything was quiet. And then a circus arrived:

Why have we stopped?
Because of the river.
Well. Let's cross it.
But how? The river's too wide.
Well, let's find a boat.
But where can we find a boat?
There's a boat over there.
But it's on the other side of the river...

Oh oh! Oh oh!
We can't get across to the other side.
Oh oh! Oh oh!
There's a very strong tide and the river's too wide.
Oh oh! Oh oh! Oh oh!

So the circus animals turned round and marched away. And at the bottom of the river the trolls laughed: No-one will ever cross this river! Ha! Ha! Ha!

Many years passed on the banks of the river. Everything was quiet. And then the miners arrived:

Why have we stopped?
Because of the river.
Well. Let's cross it.
But how? The river's too wide.
Well, let's find a boat.
But where can we find a boat?
There's a boat over there.
But it's on the other side of the river.

I know. Let's build a bridge.
But how?
With iron and steel and a lot of hard work!

So they dug and they lifted and hammered and hammered until they had built a beautiful bridge. And at the bottom of the river the trolls crawled away to hide in the mud. And they were never seen again.

Oh yeah! Oh yeah!
We *can* get across to the other side.
Oh yeah! Oh yeah!
Though there's a very strong tide and the river's too wide
This bridge will take us to the other side!
Oh yeah! Oh yeah!

Trinity Community Centre, North Ormesby

Transporter Bridge

Reaching high
above ghost masts;
vessels long gone.
Platform plying
side to side
for a hundred years.
Spanning a river
strangely silent;
no water traffic.
Remembering carts
and horses.
Glorious steel
living fossil
of a bygone age.

David Walland

Charles Twist, *100 Beats of the Clock* (photograph captured directly on to fibre paper)

It's a Boy!

He's hard and handsome,
Reliable and strong,
Steadfast and stoic.
He's a skilled craftsman
From over the Border,
A grafter, bread-winner,
A family man,
Boro born and bred.

Ormesby Library Group

Good Question

The Boro are red,
The bridge is blue,
The bridge is shut,
So what's new?!

Roy G Robertson

She

She's stood there proud for a hundred years,
Surviving two World wars,
Sturdy, proud and mighty too,
She's seen for miles in majestic blue,
From the Port of Clarence she spans the Tees,
Ferrying passengers with the greatest of ease,
Rivets, girders a gondola too,
She's Teesside's most famous view,
With a century of battling the elements,
Brushed aside with her rigid stance and elegance,
So very proud she makes us feel,
Her hundred years o'er the River of Steel.

Ian Yarrow

Everything Flows

The Transporter Bridge remembers
Streets of aunties and grandmas and cousins,
The gas-lights coming on in the evening
Beneath the canvas awnings in the market,
The aroma of stale beer and fags,
The ragamuffin kids playing outsider at all hours,
The smoke and clang and chuff and whoosh of the railways
The thud of the suicides hitting the water.

The Transporter Bridge has learned
How quickly everything changes,
How to recognise the insult of graffiti scrawl,
The bark of seals in the river,
The Saturday roar of the crowd at the Riverside,
The silver flash of a salmon's tail,
The pride of local people.

The Transporter Bridge has forgotten
The surge of crowds of men in caps,
The kids following the horses with a bucket and shovel,
The sound of the wind in the rigging of the sailing ships,
The gangs of children chasing the lamplighter,
The St Hilda's congregation in their Sunday best,
The fishy smell of the glue-factory.

The Transporter Bridge dreams
Of a windless future,
Of the Boro thrashing Chelsea,
Of busy shipping-lanes,
And a forest of cranes and new buildings rising
In a busy, growing city on the banks of the river.

Ormesby Library Group

Jean Botwright, *Transporter Bridge* (Etching)

What Does the Bridge Remember?

The old bridge still remembers:
sound of children playing on the nearby streets,
The celebrations and the sadness of the drunks,
The slap of a half-empty wage-packet on the table,
The silence of the empty houses,
The smell of smoke from the Cathedral's charred ruins,
The squeal of brakes,
The clang of the gates,
The march of feet,
The length of a late-shift,
The chatter and curses of men late for work,
The oil and smoke of the ships passing beneath,
The leaden, despairing footsteps of the midnight suicides,
The relentless imperatives of industry,
The changing, clanging shift buzzers, bells and sirens,
The ring of leather boots,
The hopes and fears of countless workers,
The stink of horses,
The power of water and wind,
The names of all the ships that sailed down the river,
The companionship of the clouds,
The silence of the sea.

Easterside Library Group

A Giant

A giant that stands both sides of the Tees,
feet firmly planted amongst the reeds.
Works hard all year round and not afraid of the cold,
this bridge of ours will stand as days grow old.
With its wings spread so wide
it could take off, but it stands here with pride
by the Tees docks.

J Horner

Just the Job

Once upon a time there was a bridge. It was a big, blue bridge. And it was a very old bridge. It was always losing things. One day the old bridge woke up. It yawned. It stretched and looked around. There was something missing. What was it? The old bridge looked and looked. Then it remembered. It used to have a job. But where was it? The bridge looked everywhere, but it couldn't find the job it used to have.

The bridge saw lots of people leaving the town.
'Hello,' said the old blue bridge. 'Where are you going?'
'We're looking for work,' they said.
'I'd better come with you,' said the old bridge.
So the old blue bridge lifted up its old blue legs and set off.

On the way the old blue bridge met a bright red oil-tanker from Saudi.
'Hello,' said the bright red oil-tanker. 'Where are you going?'
'I'm looking for a job,' said the old blue bridge.
'I thought you had a job.'
'I seem to have lost it,' said the old blue bridge. And off he went.

On the way the old blue bridge met a big fat seagull from Whitby
'Hello,' said the big fat seagull. 'Where are you going?'
'I'm looking for a job,' said the old blue bridge.
'I thought you had a job.'
'I seem to have lost it,' said the old blue bridge. And off he went.

On the way the old blue bridge met a tall white wind-turbine
'Hello,' said the tall white wind-turbine. 'Where are you going?'
'I'm looking for a job,' said the old blue bridge.
'I thought you had a job.'
'I seem to have lost it,' said the old blue bridge. And off he went.

Just then the old blue bridge heard a lot of noise. The bridge looked down. There were lots of people by the banks of the river, cheering and shouting and waving flags. There were fireworks and lights in the sky. They were waiting to cross the river!
'Happy birthday'!' the people shouted. 'Happy birthday!'

The old blue bridge smiled and turned around.
'I've found my job,' the bridge said to itself. 'It was here all the time!'

South Bank Library group

Transported

Roseberry's fin pokes through the rolling green sea
as the gondola rumbles over the River Tees,
Taking me to the Port Clarence side, where I don't alight.
I'm on a joy ride, or so it would seem, to the man
carrying the ticket machine. The truth is
I'm in search of dreams, being transported back to a time
when I was the closest my father would ever find to a son.
He's taking me to see a footy match.
His favourite team the Boro are playing.
It's a vague memory of a happy childhood
when times were hard but life was good.
It lasts the length of the return trip – gone in a flash!
Looking skyward I see the stairs we climbed just a few years ago.
They don't seem as scary from below. I wanted
to show him the world from a different view, but
as we lingered there our fingers clinging on tightly
to the blue metal rails, I think we both knew, we had drifted.
I am a branch broken free from the entangled tree
floating along with the rest of the debris
in search of new opportunities.

Chris Robinson

Jean Botwright, *Lighting the Way* (Etching)

Blue Dragon

For what does it stand?
This monument of hardships grand and staying,
Stood fast of northern winds.
By the bridge,
Once we were children playing.

What solid hand of iron heart
Then tore the hills and sky apart?
Metallic symmetry of bygone years,
Memories still bear fruit.

Of blood sweat tears this town was born.
Here now, the gates for dawn reveal anew.
By riverside, by the old man Tees,
Lay the breathing dragon blue.

Ripples in scales for valley skin,
Glint in eye of iron ore.
The hills they watched its birth,
The hills they know the score.

Born of hands, all burning dreams,
Blood the fire of life well spent.
Here let us transport ourselves,
Away from books, museum shelves.

Towards the bridge which breathes and lives,
Icon given identity to the fair folk of these lands.
Phoenix from the ashes of industry,
And still shall stand Blue Dragon,
Another hundred years and more.

And so to dream another dream,
And stand in time another year.
To transport ourselves one moment,
Inside the movement.
Towards the realization
That is our sign,
This our dragon blue,
Shall stand the test of time.
And breathe new life into this town of mine,
A town they built for you.

David Christopher Lacey

Bicycle Men of the Transporter

Giants of Men
from opposite banks
carried their bikes
above the gondola.
Between shifts
a mini Tour de France
covered the cantilevers.

Today, bungee-jumpers
hover like flies
over the water line.

Ian Horn

The Transporter

Reaching the top you stand upon a metal grid
Knees atremble on the Shimmering Way
Eyes fixed, resist the glance down at the drop,
The cross hatch shadow over slate grey water.

This bridge is a moment spanning a century
Suspending cloud from each blue girder
And a yellow gondola strung on steel sinews
Running the stream of traffic from bank to bank.

Ride the spine of the diplodocus skeleton
Frozen mid-munch on the weeds and sludge
Of muddy flats, silvered by sunshine at low tide;
On one side the marshes, wetlands to Seal Sands,

The tangle of chemical plants, then on to Seaton.
On the other the urban sprawl of terraced houses
Town centre, church spires, looming tower blocks
And the distant, hooked peak of Odinsberg –

So maybe today this bridge has become Bifrost
Connecting us to the mead hall of a one eyed
Pagan god, a raven perched on each shoulder,
Watching a longboat glide up the steel river

To plunder the hamlets of Norton and Sockburn
To nail a Saxon skin to the door of their kirk,
Hack off a Christian head or two for goblets,
And you, as ripe for picking as a Bramble

In mid-September; who once pricked a finger,
Who stubbed a bare toe and swore, who fell
Off a wall or out of a tree, who let a secret slip,
Who tossed a smooth pebble into the sea,

Who declared, 'I'll love you forever!' and meant it,
Who remembers the childish fear of the dark,
Who was once lost in a supermarket, who once
Spat 'Who the hell cares?' and refused to try,

Who over-did it at a party, threw up on the carpet,
Who once refused to admit 'I'm sorry' and then
Cried yourself to sleep; now stand wondering
If all this feeling is real, or just the blue-print

Of a human experience before construction;
Holding tight to the cold railing as you tread
This sky path to the half-way point where
Young men hurl their bodies into empty space

On threads that catch their belly roars, that churn
Your guts, and bring to mind the suicides
Who've faced the drop without a hope
Of bouncing back, and workmen who'd haul

Heavy bikes up the steep flights of steps
On bitter mornings to save a precious penny,
While industry's flames set the sky ablaze,
Rumbling like a war machine through dreams

Of local girls and boys. Today the sleepless
River takes your thoughts away, past the mothballed
Blast furnace and out to sea, with the white flash
Of a gull's wings as it banks in an effortless arc

Beneath your uncertain feet, as if it is the Herald
And you the Witness to this expanding moment –
Caught mid-point upon the Rainbow Bridge,
Listening with pricked ears to the tell-tale creak

Of tectonics; of terrains – of histories, scraping
Against one another, and holding your breath,
Like you did climbing the stairs, late at night,
Hours after the time you'd promised to be home.

Bob Beagrie

Margery Shotton, *Transporter Gate* (Watercolour on Paper)

Border Crossing

for Gordon Hodgeon

You know it well –
This point under the railway bridge
Where the past comes to haunt
As taxi repair man hammers engine
Trying to get a re-start.

You wait outside the old Customs House
Where the money was weighed
And the percentage deducted
From the sweat and mortal expiration
In these faded docklands.

The two clowns you await
Are too busy entertaining themselves
Lost on the murdered streets of St Hilda's
Trying not picture themselves
As a music hall act from
The long-gone Palace of Varieties

Their minds are loose as time's
Panic-screws tighten and they
Are suddenly an opening act –
Historical bards who can't find
A way out of the arsehole of nowhere:

An opening act for Little Tich
And his renowned Big Boot Dance
Sand-scatterers for Wilson, Kepple and Betty
Even you lose patience and go inside
Laughing at their ineptitude

As they drive round and round
clown faces as blue as the bridge that
spans the boiling river
Chanting
Transporter,
Transporter,
Transporter!

Andy Willoughby

The Transporter

For a hundred years you`ve stood
and we're proud that you`ve done us good
from being bombed in the war
we see you with awe
cos you`d have laughed if only you could.

We joke that you shut down with ease
when the wind is blowing a breeze
but it won't ruin our day
to go the long way
and use the Newport Bridge over the Tees.

So we`ll look after every nook and cranny
cos were so proud of you its uncanny ,
and we won't get upset
when we watch *Auf Wiedersehen Pet*
cos you'll always be our tranny!

Robert Instone

Blue Dog

Standing so proud
Strong, never fierce
Pretty, not passive
Symbolic of great industries past
Inspiring for their return?
A beacon on a homecoming
Advertising our spirit
Custodian of the region
Standing guard to the Towns
The 'Blue Dog', Teesside's best friend!

Gary Smith

Gillian Bradley, *Bridge #1* (Watercolour)

Metal Colossus in Blue

Way, way up there, touching the sky
With your metal fingers icy and blue.
You sparkle and shine against the black skyline.
What stories through the years you must have to tell
Straddling the Tees, like the Colossus of Rhodes, 1911 to present day,
A meeting place for lovers trysts, workers, tourists.
People on a visit to your highest place,
Climbing, abseiling from your peaks.
Raising money for good causes, the helpless and our soldier forces.
Your fame has spread far and wide,
Biggest, working, transporter bridge, worldwide.

Now, waiting for a facelift of improved flooring,
And glass lifts soaring.
Such a busy place of yesteryear.
Now the workplace and workforce around you is almost dead.
Leaving only Vulcan memories, in partial walls, brick red.
Iron, pottery, salt, shipbuilding all gone.
Nearby the clock tower, hands missing, stands formidable
As time rolls on and desolation is all around.

The water sparkles below you and a boat tipped like a drunken sailor, lolls on its side.
Lying disabled and discarded, no more a nightclub,
Where people laughed and danced the night away
Only seabirds provide the disco music now.
And the waves lap its rusty hulk.
Across the water, on both sides, stand concrete towers
And blackened chimney stacks spewing and belching still,
Flames and smoke, like a lack-lustre dragon
Filling air and nostrils with sulphur fumes.
This place, once filled with cap, clad men, in work clothes grim,
Walking and cycling to work or home,
Filling the busy transporter bridge, going back and forth
Driven by the winching crew.
Cycles slung over riders shoulders, cheaper to climb the metal steps
Saves pennies for the day.
Walking the length of the metal blue, no fear of heights allowed
And God, what a view.

Further down the river, once dockland, filled with boats and ships
Seamen going about their business of the day
Later, seeking satisfaction with the dock girls of the night.
All this is gone, lost in the swirling mists of time
With loss of jobs, loss of pay, a heritage mislaid.

But walking down, once busy Vulcan Street,
Seen in the distance is another giant mass, of iron and sparkling mesh.
A Diablo, balanced on rods of steel
A work of art, 'Temenos' by name, keeping the blue transporter encircled in its frame
And sings when the wind blows through.
It represents all that's new.
Teesside regenerating, mixing old with the new.
And of all this change, the transporter blue, silently keeps an overview.

Irene Styles

Transported

for Liz

I didn't try it with my lover,
didn't visit with my kids,
never brought my Southern mother,
I came here with my good friend Liz.

And as we rode across the river,
she told me about the Clarences men –
a 12 hour shift at the Britannia steelworks,
then walking home across the top to save the fare.

I've always been a fan of the bizarre, the clever,
things that are a bit out of their time,
structures no longer fit for purpose,
but holding on, reminding us of other days.

And what I really like, what's most ironic,
the fact that if they hang on long enough,
they can achieve a status that's iconic
become a national treasure to be preserved.

Marilyn Longstaff

Gillian Bradley, *Bridge #2* (Watercolour)

The Transporter

Give it the 'Grand Coullee Dam'
give it the Guthrie;
glorify the working man
more than Connaught Arthur.

Invited to the opening
he wore civil vestments
of an 'in loco' make-do king
in Saville Row sartoria.

He functioned, like the gondola
slung on high flung rails,
strung like a massive mandola
tuned for percussive clacks.

Give it the 'Grand Coullee Dam'
give it the Guthrie
Glorify the working man
more than Connaught Arthur.

Glorify the gib-crank swings
balancing hornby girders;
north and south the sloping wings
helped fashion unique shape.

Besting Runcorn's finials,
Newport, Gwent's skeletal
syntax interlineal
geometric splendour.

Give it the 'Grand Coullee Dam'
give it the Guthrie
Glorify the working man
more than Connaught Arthur.

Coming and going normal,
Lowry in technical,
to schedule and informal
hammers rivet rivets.

On the teeming river banks
eggs, bacon, black pudding
in blackened cauldrons on the flanks
fried in axle grease.

Alan E Watkiss

Home Run

Dressed in khaki and shades of blue
heroes home from foreign fields
eager to see a yellow harvest
and friendly ships along the coast
find a place on the hanging ferry
as she heaves her way across the Tees
from the 'Boro to the Port.

A soldier leans into the iron gates,
stares into the whipped green swell
and thinks back to a schoolboy
his eyes closed, anticipating the sting
of the salty spray on his face, as the ferry
heaves her way across the Tees
from the 'Boro to the Port.

Inside her gingham café Florrie waits
while water boils. Her heroes will sit
on wooden stools at high counters
and smoke Woodbines from green packets
and talk of familiar things, as the ferry
heaves her way across the Tees
from the 'Boro to the Port.

From the gantry, a warning bell sounds a safe crossing.
Into the marking bay the silent ferry floats,
carried over tarry nets, wet and dry walls tell of high and low tides.

Monica Sharp

M for Middlesbrough

She stands aloof, haughty and proud,
a monumental M,
proclaiming her own history.
The steel tart of Middlesbrough.

Once she took mariner's commerce
between her outstretched legs,
but now she's only a short cut,
to another bank,
a tourist curio.

Not accommodating,
like hunch backed Newport,
nor gracefully slender,
like upstream Victoria,
or the new, Princess Diana.
Hers is a beauty,
which flows from the hands that made her.

Under her pale blue dress,
of light and paint,
her bare legs show,
one on either bank,
hedging her bets,
waiting,
for the next trick of fate.

Brian Morton

Ode to the Transporter

Twin peaks of Teesside,
Majestic and blue
Back in the 50s
I first knew you.
Day at the seaside,
Seaton Carew
Take the transporter
And a bus ride too.
I remember the catch net,
Ominous below,
How many cars fell,
You'll never know
A clank and a rumble
Then off it would go
I'd run to the front
You could see the Tees flow.
A brave teenager
I climbed to the top
It took quite some courage
It's really some drop.
You mean so much to me,
I feel a great pride
Spanning the river
So big and so wide.
Fond memories
Blue in the night
If they try to close you
They're in for a fight!

Norma Guy

Branded

Not long ago, before you were even a tiny little logo,
I would watch for your ham-fisted scribble in the
sulphur-scented sky.
We couldn't care less if you were Art or Graffiti,
back then; just a God-given, indelible
marker of territory too raw to own.

My daughter can only recognise you window-dressed
In azure – a twenty-four/seven, mixed
media mannequin.
It is true that your cobalt cuts an aesthetic
dash against their midnight. So does the waxy
imprint of a gull crashing into crystal.

Not so long ago, before 'M' meant super-sized,
Globalised arches, you spanned the Tees, unspun.
The only way was
steel grey. Putting pen to blotting-paper promises,
we practised solid signatures, not indigo
autographs in invisible, electric ink.

Helen Victoria Anderson

The Brollys of Boro

In praise of a Transport of Delight

Like the skeleton of a giant Edwardian umbrella,
a proper brolly made from fabricated steel and built to last,
Normandy blue, illuminated on the Tees night sky-line,
Transporter – it is time you were the star of a romantic film.

If Jacques Demy could do it for your feeble cousin
in *Les Parapluies de Cherbourg*, 1964, it's time
that you were rescued from a bit part in a Geordie sitcom,
and your silent real-life role in Terry Scott's decline.

You deserve a major Oscar-winning director,
a megastar of Catherine Deneuve fame,
all the drama of her love-sick shop girl,
and music, dancing, brollys, singing in the rain.

Marilyn Longstaff

Gillian Spensley, *The North East's Greatest* (Acrylic on Canvas)

Transporter

in memory of Charlie O' Neill 1905-2007

You didn't go so far.
Borne across the tracks
from Thornaby
and back to your chair
in time for the TV and
the match

girls striking out. 1905.
It is before you are a young man

stubborn old sod

you shake my uncertain hand
from the nineteen twenties
between the foundry

and somewhere

your sister still
scrambling for that one pound note
she let inadvertently fly
into air.

Michael Brown

Our Transporter

Our Transporter,
Effortlessly straddling the water
The lifeblood of the town
The Tees,
Dominating the skyline
Of The Infant Hercules.

Built of steel and might
Lit up blue in the night
All there for us to see
One hundred years of glory .

Gary Wake

Sanctuary

Two bony, Meccano birds
Each side of river,
Neck-deep in mud,
Love divided, it's
Drawn into a kiss.
So beak tips meet
And fuse. A symbol
Of their passion,
Flesh stripped,
Raw as iron,
They carry the weight,
The world's burden.
Both shiver
In the slight sway.
Their mutual bond.
Their belonging
At this crossing place,
Together.

Gordon Hodgeon

Transport us for a Century

The transporter is our history
It's never let us down
It has seen two world wars
It's our jewel in the crown

It stands as strong as ever
It's tall and proud and great
It stands for all that's Teesside
To our county it's the gate

For myself it's a bit more daring
So I climbed right to the top
Put elastic round my ankles
To enjoy a massive drop

I raised cash for comic relief
Buts that is not all
I loved the whole experience
I really had a ball

So forget our modern gadgets
Computers and mobile phones
Our transporter has seen it all
It tells us we are home!

A hundred great years it's been here
As the years have come and gone
It never ever lets us down
When all is said and done

So raise a glass to our history
For it still is standing here
And for the next hundred years
Let us all give a huge cheer!

Karen Raby

Her Heart May Beat of Iron

Her heart may beat of iron,
Her Soul may sing of steel,
Yet her voice! Invisible and silent to many,
To Teesside and Cleveland sounds so real.

To cross her is what we do,
Night and day,
Has many times as possible,
She wouldn't have it any other way.

She may not be London Bridge, or the Eiffel Tower,
The statue of Liberty or even the Hollywood sign.
To the people of Teesside and Cleveland,
She is simply, and always will be –
A bridge too far.

Peter de Dee

Not Just a Physical Structure

It was one time ago a miracle
Bridging two sides from two separate identities
Ways of life destined to cross paths allowed by the structure
Once desolate then came an industry champion complete
Man made translating the mechanisms of industrial change
A unity created from the bridging of the gap
As a child every now and then
In my granddad's car we went
Across the river on a structure that transported all races all divides
It was a mode of unity that encompassed everybody
With no discriminatory sources of alienation
The bridge that in essence links one side to the other
Where the industrial revolution spread its mobility spanning over many countries.
What is its destiny, I guess for now the bridge is safe
But where has the industry settled or has it has its day.
To many the industry that created this bridge of late
Is the same bridging source of enterprise that translates endeavour?
Or has the focus gone from the mastering of engineering protocol?
The transporter bridge remains in its glory
But the industry that creates such mechanisms is another story
The steel industry and the engineers are rebuking the grain
Bringing back the same question again and again.
Will we ever build another marvel like this
The bridging of a unity for all sides of it to gain.
The know how remains but so too does the emergence of cost effective ways
Today's glory is tomorrows history
Yesterdays production expressing connectivity
Not just a structure then it concerns everybody
The holistic elements to the production of a bridge
Not just a manufactured bridge alone it has hidden depths of understanding.
The Transporter Bridge.

Robert Alan Cowley

Across the Bridge to the Seaside

Looking back as a child I can remember
the ride across the Tees on our way to the seaside.
The ride in the car towards the town centre,
the site in the distance of that blue iconic steel statue.
My dad saying that people used to walk over there
trying to remember the pictures of men in bowler hats.
The gate crashing, open the excitement in my stomach,
the bumps beneath the car.
The blue steel that stretches up forever and into the sky,
the cables you can hear them stretch as the movement rattles to a start.
The suspended gliding through the air,
the wind blowing around my face whistling its way along the Tees.
The man asking for money to pay for the journey,
my dad looking for change.
The journey itself doesn't last long as we jump back into the car.
The promise of the long sunny seaside day ahead
with the bucket and spade in the boot.
The rattling starts and the cars start to depart
as the man opens the yellow gates.
I remember looking back at the mass blue machine
and thinking when we will do it again.
I now drive the car with the child in the back asking to be taken across.
I wonder how she will see it,
I wonder what she will think.
I wonder if she will shout 'transporter' whenever she sees it.

Garry Morrison

Limerick

The Transporter Bridge is fantastic,
Made or iron and steel, not plastic,
It crosses the Tees
With the greatest of ease,
Like it's on a big length of elastic.

Pat Avent

The Lady of the Tees

Some say Cook put the town on the map
others say Bolckow or Pease
but it's not been a man who's been steadfast in our making
its a ladyship bridge o' forged metal, cast on the banks o' the Tees
for one hundred years the lady's been smiling
surveying t' stack and the apse with some ease
when you come on to Teesside give a nod in her direction,
the old lady, she's the gateway to the north seas
there's nothing this woman hasn't encountered
navigator and quaker and captive, speculator, rigger and steam
below in her apron they've busied, the coal and iron 'n' slack

so stand... raise a glass... in time honoured tradition
salute! To the Middlesbrough Transporter
'the past we inherit, the future we build'
its the message from our world famous mechanical daughter.

Garry Hassell

Cerulean

cerulean set against stormy space
uprights and horizontals
your angles define this place

chimneys and rooftops patiently await
a grey clothed workforce
crossing over just to put food on the plate

a daily migration from south to north
the men of the Boro
bringing a bright industrial future forth

time passed by but the vision faded
erosion set in
tumbleweed blows through factories degraded

here where ironworks and shipyards thrived
time moved on
Teesside waits for the good times to be revived

form over function you became
a symbolic icon to be proud
a landmark to behold with popular acclaim

Keith Sell

Stronger Together

Me Grandad's bridge is that –
Climbed over the top twice daily
To get to the docks,
Or so he told me.

Me Dad's bridge is that –
On hands and knees he fixed
The motor right on top,
Or so he told me.

Me Mam's bridge is that –
Came over from the wrong
Side of the river,
Or so she told me.

My bridge is that –
Made of bright blue steely steel
Whose loving arms reveal
What I, you, we all feel –

Stronger together.

Harry Gallagher

The Scream

If I was at the top of the Transporter Bridge
I would scream a hundred times,
Each scream would mean that it has been There for a hundred years,
If I was falling off the Transporter Bridge I'd probably scream again (and again and again!),
If I was at the bottom of the Transporter Bridge I wouldn't scream at all,
If I was going across the Transporter Bridge I wouldn't scream again.

Ben Hodgson

Adrian Moule, *Transporter Bridge* (Oil on Canvas Board 12" x 10")

The Transporter Bridge

One hundred years on and still going strong,
It was built to last, you see,
Built by people like you and me,
Or was it?
Hard graft, pride and pleasure,
Constructed a national treasure,
Symbol of a nation, proud and strong,
A nation too belong,
One hundred years on,
What's gone wrong?

Nothing is built to last,
Not many working at doing their best,
Idly watching a nation crash,
Not a very pleasant sight to see.

Meanwhile the old Tranny grabs my hand
And tries to lead me back,
An impossible task, but I try to understand
The span between 1911 and 2011,
Even the nickname doesn't sound the same.

As for me,
I crossed the River Tees on the Tranny when
Each day was filled with hard graft, pride and pleasure,
Dare I ask, will there ever be such like again,
I think, maybe never,
Which makes me glad,
I was born when I was.
Just in time to see the old Tranny still thriving
On hard graft, pride and pleasure.

Robert Lonsdale

Recipe for a Bridge

First take an act of parliament
Bung in a load of metal
Add some steel
And a cup of kindness
In a well greased mould,
Stir in some hard work,
Crack in some sun and people
Shake in blue pigment
And some iron for good measure,
Mix in hard work,
And a sprinkling of Boro,
Add some postcard views
Pour in tons of water
Dunk it in blue icing and leave for 100 years…

The Boro Buzz

Bridge Haikus

Pretty epic heights
But they don't scare me at all
How could you be scared?

Blue metal monster
Clanking and clunking, bright light
Small reflections move.

Towering Metal
Gondola moving under
Light and sun dancing.

It stands so proudly
The very first bridge of its kind
Awesome views from top.

The Boro Buzz

On The Money

Once it had been just an Idea, as these things
simply Are, Platonic, born in one man's brain,
while shaped as these things must be – were in 1873 –
by the paradigms of a new age of Steam
and Coal and Iron. Smith's Dream

come to nothing, because these things snare
on Committees, cf Council Meeting, March 6, 1906,
Councillor Allison: 'A Showman Enterprise'.
Councillor Sadler: 'Throwing money in the wind,'
also 'The ratepayer's burden', and so on –

and a fine Idea fell, as these things have to fall,
     into
         the quotidian,
               spent time
                      as these things must,
     with tiresome ambitions   paltry calculations
    mired among accountants   smeared with toil –
     came down
         at last to costings:
               the money maelstrom,
annualrevenueexpected£70interestof5%for40yrs
atacostof£3,000plus othercosts£1,600pacontingency
margin£2,40fundedbylocalmoney construct
ioncost£68,026 6 8d.
        Inevitably, as Big Ideas will –

      then   found
    a shape again   forged in iron,
  and maybe money talked, just this one time, a local lingo
 people understood, and an Idea came to town, and made itself at home;
came to be inevitable, celebrated, as these things always should be; rarely are.

Ann Graal

Mary Hicks, *Crossing to the Works* (Watercolour on Paper)

Our Day in the Sun

'We shall be,'
Or so the saying goes,
The rise of Hercules foretold.

What does it mean,
To be not yet?
No commander of men,
Just a hopeful cadet.
To be no thriving flower,
But a promising shoot?
The first sign of spring
With industrial roots.

Is to rise one day,
All we can hope?
No reference to time,
Nor manner, nor scope?
We wait still as one,
For the day we rise,
With faithful hearts,
And bleary eyes.

But look at the river – does that bridge not show –
We worked, we built, we grew, we rose?

Sean Barnes

Transporter

A wonderful steel structure,
Magnificent in blue,
It's been here for a hundred years,
Can stand another two,
A landmark for the area,
A work of art that's visible to all,
Steel wrought by men,
And fashioned for us all.

Kevin Stephenson

A Hundred Years Ago

A hundred years ago on a cold Tuesday,
The royal prince Albert came to say,
'I do now declare this bridge open.'
But it is now one of less than ten.

This famous landmark of our small town,
As a Grade 2 listing it will never come down,
From Middlesbrough to Port Clarence
To walk along the top took great balance.

So celebrate we must do with style,
To plan it right will take a while,
Who knows, perhaps another prince will come,
Not as old as the last, a younger one.

RG Phillips

The School Run

Peeling potatoes in the sun
Two doors down from Carroll's pub
She squints up as her youngest son
Tarzan-calls, then starts his run
Down, skittering, daft as a marble,
Bouncing her heart off the treads with him,
In her mouth, in her boots, as he flickers
Through the flights, his Grammar School sock-cuff-hoops
Blue-and-white, blue-and-white, blue-and-white

Liz Geraghty

Big Blue and Strong

I am the Transporter, big, blue and strong.
A lot of my friends have now long gone,
Friends I grew up with, all of that time,
Friends who looked up to me, covered in grime.
I looked over Cannon Street, I watched the kids grow,
And the pubs on the corners, where the adults would go,
Old Wesleyan chapel and Hugh Bell School,
Gilke Street Baths with its lovely green pool,
Exchange Buildings, a kind of a martyr,
A very close neighbour of the Star and Garter,
Jordison printers, Tower House and Baum's,
Two World Wars when I dodged the bombs,
And the old infirmary, a good mate of mine.
I ask myself why, time after time,
Why did they let my good friends go?
They were the seeds that helped the town grow,
So many of my friends have now long gone,
I stand in their memory, big, blue and strong.

Paul Adamson

I Stand Proud

I stand proud in the midnight sky,
People look up in awe as they pass by.
My structure is bold, shiny and blue,
Flashing other colours if Johnny wants it to!
The river Tees beautiful and wide,
No problem! My gondola carries
Vehicles and people to the other side.
I've stood here for a hundred years,
'Stood the test of time',
Go on! Have a good look. You can tell!
Those men who built me, built me well.

Janet Jeffrey

Alan Morley, *La Middlesbrough Dance. (Homage to Matisse)* (Oil on board)

Unbecoming

Everyone's climbing up to the top of the Transporter
Singing, beaming. You'd think they were kids, to look that happy,
But it's everyone, everybody you know's there

Belting out Boro anthems and R Kelly
From the Port side there's even a few chanting Latin
Salve Regina drowning I Believe I Can Fly

And the mayor's standing by, well-cronied, taking the credit.
Snaps for the *Gazette* and bites for the BBC
This extraordinary event, this popular uprising

Men and women hauling themselves above what they're afraid of
Using a spindly prop that's mostly made of air
And the great motto, '*Erimus*' looking for completion

A smart car with dark glass holds itself apart.
If there's a senior spook inside, swapping Morrissey gigs
With the suit in that helicopter, you wouldn't know.

They are all de Brus when they reach the high gangway
Owning the hills and Cleveland plain and everything they see
They're unable ever to forget this moment

Unless the quick long fall down is a form of forgetting,
Unbecoming, in the tease.

Liz Geraghty

Transporter Bridge

Today we learned in school
About a thing called the Transporter Bridge.
It's a bridge that transports.
(A bit obvious, don't you think?)

I might just go and visit it,
After a game of tennis.
It must be somewhere in Italy
(Aren't gondolas in Venice?)

Gina Brennan

Transporter

I am known by many names
Giant dragonfly, some unkindly
Call me Meccano but
'The Tranny' those love me call
Left foot in St. Hilda
Right in Port Clarence
I straddle the river Tees
Like Gulliver
Among race of Lilliputians
Gulliver of steel
To bear Witness
To the work and toil of
Multitude, who flocked
From all corners of the world
Grateful to be an opportunity
To feed hungry mouths.

Day and night
Long shifts
The Ironmen toiled
Darkened days
Set nights blaze
In place of a hamlet
An Ironopolis grew,
Made ships, railways
And bridges
Earned Ironmasters untold riches
To feed hungry mouths.

For nearly a century
Hungry mouths were fed
But one day politicians decided
Coalminers were getting too big for their boots
Unions had to brought into line
Broke the back of iron making of Teesside
The new Ironmaster
In searched of cheap labour and
Greater profit

Left quietly to third world countries
Taking away the bread and butter
Used to feed hungry mouth.

The River is silent
No steel, no shipyards
The symbol of industry
Replaced by places of learning
And service industries
Steel making –
Has faded memory
And is only for history books
But I the Transporter
Whatever they call me at time
When the bones of the Ironmen's
Children's children are dust
They shall gaze upon me, the
Witness of the Ironmen toil
To feed hungry mouths.

Khadim Hussain

The Transporter

The majestic river Tees dinosaur
Across nearly 600 feet it does soar,
Spanning over the might north river,
Middlesbrough's road links to deliver.

Erected just a mere century ago,
Across the peat-stained water's flow,
Built with rivets, sweat, iron and steel,
Forged with pride all Teessider's feel.

A sight admired from both near and far,
Crossing the waters on a gondola,
|Lit up at night now in shades of blue,
A bridge unique, left just one of a few.

Ted Hardwick

A Century in Blue

Craig Hornby was inspired
In *A Century in Stone*
When wealthy Ironmasters
Made Middlesbrough their own.

A time for making iron
When miners dug with stealth
Their souls now long forgotten
In illusions of great wealth.

The groaning of the hillsides
When skies turned red at night
A never ending process
A truly awesome sight.

The boom brought many thousands
To venture to the Tees
A bridge would be essential
To help them cross with ease.

A moving carriage cradle
To make the journey shorter
So they agreed to build it
Then call it 'The Transporter'.

Now sense the pride of Teesside
When you look up to the sky
For the spirit of our fathers
Is a wonder to the eye.

Salute a Centenarian
Commanding such a view
A great legacy to Teesside:
A Century in Blue.

Fred Jones

The Transporter Bridge

The Transporter Bridge is an icon of our town,
Because of its type, it's worldwide renowned;
She is the only working one of her kind,
She's mechanical, but there's nothing to wind.

Transporting cars over the Tees since 1911,
Standing tall reaching upwards to heaven,
Now she's in her centenary year,
She's one hundred years old and needs lots of care.

She has worked all her life, a tribute we know,
Lit up at night she takes on a blue glow,
Loved by the people, the lady of Middlesbrough town,
It if was possible we would be given a crown.

Alan Brownbridge

On a Visit to the Transporter Bridge

Said a lad to his dad, 'Why make it so high?'
Said dad, 'That's to let the tall ships go by.
Ships passed by here hundreds each way
To Thornaby, Stockton, and out to Tees Bay.'
'Why, Dad,' said the lad, 'Did they make it so wide?'
'Well, now. It's to reach right over the tide.
Folks lived on one bank but worked on the other.
It moved man and his wife, the sister and brother
Some rode the Gondola and paid for the ride.
Some climbed the ladders, a matter of pride
To race up the steps, on over the track,
Carrying their bicycles over their backs
Then down again, taking more care.
They'd beaten their mates and saved their fare.'

Jane Dunn

Transporter

Seen from a distance,
Radiant blue against night sky,
Focussing attention, concentrating eye
On hot riveted elegant form.
Tall tapering towers soaring
Rise skywards on opposite banks,
Multifingered hinged topped
To support hunchbacked cantilevers
Issuing out from either shore,
Pivoted, firm-stayed, to ride
Fierce stress excess, supporting
Multi-wheeled carriage, suspended
Platform on tensile steel cables,
Positively pulled reciprocatingly
By powerful winch anchored firm
On Yorkshire bank shuttling
Lorries, cars, pedestrians, all
To Durham, across broad Tees
Keeping open the river
For clipper ships from overseas!

Keith Porritt

          Immense changes I perceive
   Nobody envisaged these changes within our environment
     Bygone   The
     year's   boundaries
     are history   and
     since   increasing
     development   population
     and reconstruction   starting
              Middlesbrough's recreation.

GR Bennison

Dee Maloney, *Blue Sky over the Transporter Bridge* (Print)

The Transporter Bridge

For a hundred years
This grand old lady has stood,
Spanning the Tees,
Through the bad times and the good.

Connecting communities
In the North and the South,
What stories she could tell
Straight from the river's mouth.

The magnificent gondola
Gracefully glides above the river,
Her cargo and passengers
Safely to deliver.

Two thousand six hundred tons
Of Teesside steel,
Transformed from an idea
To a structure so real.

Now a famous landmark,
For our town to be proud,
The Transporter Bridge is amazing –
So shout it loud!

Kayla McBride

I Stand

I stand here alone on the howling wind,
I taste the moisture in the fresh, salty air,
World wars and women's rights are yesterday to me.
I remember my youthful years,
Long, long ago now.
I hold people's lives in the balance.
I creak with age.
I grin when they jump off me.
I weep as the men who made me pass away.
I sleep when the lights go out.

Kathryn Mellor

Down the Ferry Road

1948. I am eight years old.
The riverside is my adventure playground.
We swarm like ants
Foraging in the dead rail tracks,
Scavenging for anything of interest to take home.

I take myself off
to visit the Transporter Bridge.
I dawdle, my eyes following the cradle
As it hums methodically through the grey mist.
I stand well clear of the barriers,
And when those clanging jaws crunch onto land
There is a storm of working men charging through the gates
With an effusion of grunts, shouts and banter,
Shoving and pushing for elbowroom
As they surge forward,
Desperate to get on the first bus.

The river is awash with oil,
Moving like molasses,
Smelling of turps.
In the distance above the skyline,
The chimneys belch black and white smoke across the Tees.
The furnaces stink.
Dock Street is foggy with gas.
Above me, huge cranes swing
Their heavy cargoes across the leaden sky.
The boneyard gives off its offensive smell,
An invisible cloud sneaking into the streets and houses.

Colleen Batey

Beloved Tranny

Our Transporter Bridge across the Tees,
Makes us Teessiders proud and at ease,
The Tranny Bridge as it's known to many,
To cross it used to cost a penny.

Built over a hundred years ago,
It stands so tall, through hail, rain and snow,
The Tranny is known worldwide,
It's the symbol of home – it's Teesside.

No matter where you travel or where you roam,
To see the Transporter means you are home,
The Transporter Bridge is home to me,
It will stay in my heart for eternity.

Keith Kirkbride

The Blue Lady of the Tees

As I take my son and daughter
Over the Tees
Aboard the Transporter,

The giant towers skyward bound,
This huge metal structure
With minimal sound

Glides over the water.
The look of delight
From my son and my daughter!

Anyone who has seen her
Is truly smitten,
She's the oldest of her type
In the whole of Britain.

Who would have thought
Or placed a bet
On this grand old lady
Stealing the show
On *Auf Wiedersehen Pet*!

Mick Crosby

Mega-Meccano

I had a Meccano as a boy,
I'd say it was my favourite toy,
Miniature girders and metal bits,
Finding out where everything fits.

As a child I hadn't been to Middlesbrough,
I came here in 2006, you know!
I'm a lad from Yorkshire through and through
Who found himself in pastures new.

I have always been one who liked exploring,
And I found summat I could not be ignoring,
There it was – a Meccano supreme,
The biggest one I'd ever seen!

I stood watching cards fly through the air,
On wires they just dangled there.
It's a great way to go across the Tees,
To end up in Hartlepool with ease.

It's a priceless treasure, beyond compare,
The quickest way from here to there,
You won't encounter a traffic jam,
And be late for your tea and upset your Mam!

Anthony Gibson

Alone

I see the boats sailing past,
The bright sun setting on the sleepy town.
Another century passes me by,
Still stood here, all alone.

No-one to share the breathtaking view with,
(Apart from the birds, and they are not here very long):
The dusky sunsets and morning blues,
The first evening star above orange skies,
Still stood here, still alone.

Elinor Northey

Notice to the Good People of Port Clarence Concerning Middlesbrough's New Transporter Bridge

Prone once to Viking slaughter,
Not victor in things sportier,
The Boro lies, her football team
Supported by the creamiest cream
Of Middlesbrough.

Not made with bricks and mortar,
Colossus-like, but haughtier,
It waits, Transporter of Delight,
To bring you on dull days and bright
To Middlesbrough.

A newspaper reporter
(Truth-teller, no distorter)
Declared up on its opening day,
'This is the wisest warmest way
To Middlesbrough'.

Who dare not walk on water,
Have faith in the Transporter,
'Twill bear you dry-shot, when you please,
Above the tide's tumultuous Tees
To Middlesbrough.

To send a son or daughter
'cross rivers long or shorter,
Construct a gondola by wires
Suspended from celestial spires.
Like Middlesbrough.

Philip Holt-Swain

Glittering Gorgeously

The beautiful, big, blue bridge,
Glittering gorgeously
Above the shimmering shiny water.

Ellie Stephenson

Twin Towers

There's a clang of the metal gate closing,
Workmen all huddled together on board,
From a distance it looked like a magic carpet
As across the river it soared.

Thousands of workmen have travelled
Cloth caps and boots hobnailed,
Dodging the boats on the river
Where hundreds of ships have sailed.

Working in the old foundries,
Fettling the things they make,
It may seem like Dante's inferno,
But it's only our flesh that they bake.

You can look back in our history
About a hundred years ago,
When the Transporter was erected
And it's still on show.

It looks like a magic carpet,
Hanging loose beneath the span
Can the wires hold it?
You bet your life they can!

How many miles of travel
I wouldn't dare to say,
Doing over a hundred trips
Every working day.

Built by Teesside craftsmen,
It has stood the test of time,
Gleaming in the sunlight,
It really does look fine.

Our massive metallic monster
Fills us all with pride,
Like pterodactyl's kissing,
Stretching from each side.

Peter Nolan

Bungee Jumping off the Transporter

The sky is an elephant, ramming the clouds,
The river below is a mist, murky and dark,
On your right is Port Clarence,
A town of ghosts and memories,
On your left is Middlesbrough,
Dolls' houses and toy cars,
The glass bottle,
Cardboard cut-out flats,
Cloud-making factory chimneys,
And giraffe-like cranes bending and swinging,
A rainbow splash of colours,
The glittering bowl of the sea,
And beyond the sea the dark outline of the horizon,
Stretching out like the edge of the world…

You are on the edge of a cliff.
You stand on the edge and close your eyes.
You can't look down.
Your breathing is heavy.
You are in a nightmare.
You feel like you are going to be sick.
No time for regrets now.
There is no going back.
You are terrified and excited.
A butterfly is eating your stomach.
You want to be sick.
Your whole life pauses.
And then, with a burst of courage, you drop…

You are falling, flying,
Spinning, tumbling,
Your insides are churning,
Your head is spinning,
Your brain is going to come out of your nose,
All the blood is rushing to your head,
Your eyes feel like they are going to pop,
You have left your stomach behind,
An anaconda is crushing the breath out of your lungs,

Your body is going to shut down,
You feel like you are going to die,
As your whole life flashes before you.
The wind is freezing,
You can hear lightning flashing,
The wind is crashing in your head,
All your emotions are blended in one concoction of fear,
You are a rocket from outer space,
A meteor falling to earth,
A tiny drop of water falling from the sky,
A ghost, a bird, hanging gracefully in mid-air.
Time slows down,
You are in a dream,
You are falling to earth in slow-motion,
The river is a mysterious whirlpool pulling you down,
You are falling into the curvaceous arms of the river,
Beautiful and translucent,
You are falling into the river's wide mouth.
The water is rushing towards you!
You are going to hit it!

Suddenly the bungee pulls you back up –
Boing! Boing! Boing!
You are on a trampoline,
A bouncy castle in the air,
Springing up and down, up and down,
Like a yoyo,
Like a puppet on a string.
You just hang there.
You are crying,
You can't believe it,
It's over!
You did it!
You did it!

Overfields Primary School

Alan Morley, *The River Tees at Middlesbrough, 1911* (Oil and Pencil on Board)

Our True Centurion

On Teesy's riverside, mulling o'er times long gone,
My eyes tango in this now lost land of life, oh dear
I murmur, idolized places, 'where did they go?'
The railway, towers, tools, once brought alive by men of grit and valour.
Behind me was a sunny cornfield that held its shade in all weathers,
Now there's route posts pointing folk everywhere
And hills we rolled held kids in jolly sounds, morning till night.

Squatter huts are mirage where we used to hide,
From there we'd see bridgeman crossing flags
Till boat sallied outa sight, then down iron steps
Perhaps to sound 'foghorn', which reminds me –
Where is ould 'foggy' in this day and age?

Still, our Teesy's calm till a mighty flap disturbs
Birds, salmon, otters have party dived for snappers
In slimy shiny coats, why's everything changed to very new
Leaving nowt sacred, not anything we can do.
Even grassy lay-bys show caras to prize our eyes
Wi' dogs, whose barks are worse than one's bite I'm told,
But still you walk on looking over your shoulder
Thinking, 'everything that glitters isn't gold.'

Then glory piece, Tranny shows a bedded truth of eternity
Remained firm, regal, in its own town for a century
Aye! A true centurion who's seen around here before I;
I would love his opinion on our many changing throes,
But as silence stalls between us, I guess I'll never know.

Joan Clark

Majestic

Transporter Bridge all blue & majestic,
But should the wind blow, it's never electric,
Cause when the wind blows, it's kind of eccentric.

Martin Fletcher

The Sense of a Bridge

I stand alone and watch the world evolve,
One hundred years have I lived and breathed.
I am unbowed
But my senses are weakened.
I watch the world fulfil its destiny,
Each person different in every aspect,
I taste the rust in my joints.
I feel the wind in my bones,
Tormenting the birds' flight pattern,
I hear the clang and clinks of locking metal joints,
I smell the stink of dying industry.

Sam Power

The Transporter Bridge

This is a bridge that we can use
To cross the deep, dark river.

These are the barriers
That stop us from falling
Into the deep, dark river.

Sometimes she swings,
Sometimes she's still,
Above the deep, dark river.

This is a bridge that we can use
To cross the deep, dark river.

Luke Williams

The Big Blue Bridge

We come from the shadows of the big blue bridge

I'm a wing-runner, I'm a bare-back bad boy,
I'm a parmo-muncher, I'm a funky mover,
I'm a freedom worker

We come from a place where you can
Ride down mud hills on your arse
It feels like a bomb must have dropped there
Kids are mad on bikes and scooters
Cheeky as, hear them swear
Drinking and acting hard everywhere!

We come from the shadows of the big blue bridge

Watch out for the bag-heads all around
Trying to score for just a few pounds
There's our big blue bridge. The only thing that's good
It's made of metal and not from wood
It's too big to twock – you can't weigh it in
If you jump off with a bungee rope
You won't need to swim

We come from the shadows of the big blue bridge

Now look over there at the rusty metal shed
Horses run by but the community farm is dead
Remember riding bareback across the green fields
Through rustling litter and how it made you feel

We come from the shadows of the big blue bridge

Listen to the raving tunes blasting from the ruins
The kids are desperate dancers avoiding parents and school
Dodging street wardens and the local PC

We come from a place where people dis single mums
But its stay away dads who are the real bums
We come from a place where your mates stick close
When the Port see the Billogs they never run away
Watch out for the boyos coming your way!

Cos we come from the shadows of the big blue bridge.

A Way Out/ARC

The River Grave

Rolling in the river, out here in the cold and dark,
Here comes another body,
Floating sadly in the water
Like an old, mouldy dead log.
I start to shake,
But I have to hook it onto my boat.
I try not to look,
As I lure it and tug it towards me:
A pale, fat body, bloated and hairy,
Miserable and melancholy,
Lurking in the water like a piece of dirt,
The flotsam and jetsam of the river.
Who was she? Why did she do it?
I try not to look at her eyes
But they draw me closer,
Pale and shiny as the moon.
The eyes hypnotise me.
The salty tears shine on my face like stars,
Cold in the freezing early morning light.
The body stink of rotting fish,
the arms are covered in small bit marks.
The body rolls over and sighs,
A mournful and despondent sound.
She looks at me, as if to say,
'Help me! Save me! Bury me!
Save me from this watery and weeping grave!'
I grit and grind my teeth and row for shore,
Rolling in the water
Beneath the old Transporter.

Pennyman Primary School

Holding On

I couldn't let go as I climbed the first step
I told them I hated heights
But they laughed and urged me on.

I couldn't let go as I reached the first landing
Two hands as I turned and 'don't look down'
A brave smile on my lips
As I pretended to be 'enjoying the challenge'

A long, long pause half way up
As others came down
Should I join them? Pretend I had been all the way up?
But my friends were waiting
I couldn't give up

No more steps but a ladder
I couldn't let go
Nor stop myself from fearing the downward descent

Then the top – what a view
And how wide it was up there
'just like a pier'
But still I couldn't let go

The sun blazed on
It was calm and still
A distant cheer rose from the stadium
Echoed by those on the bridge
I punched the air with my free hand
With the other, I couldn't let go.

The downward spiral
Close your eyes and hang on
Think of England or at least of the Boro
And whatever you do, don't let go

Terra firma at last and my legs like jelly
But a glow inside. I had done it and survived.
I looked back at my bridge
Paint blue meets sky blue
I'll come back again
I don't want to let go.

Janet Lancefield

Dennis Roddam, *Transporter Triptych* (Painted Tiles)

Transporter Bridge

The Transporter Bridge is big and blue,
It shimmers on the water, strong and true.

It stands tall and proud,
So shout it loud,

Let's sing a song or two –
For what would we do

Without this big blue crossing machine?

Victoria Dolan

The Opening of the Transporter

This is the tale of what happened
When they opened the famous Transporter,
And a really posh chap in a big tall top hat
He slipped and he fell in the water.

When the cradle moved over the river
He fell back and he opened the gate,
He tried to catch grip of the rail
But alas, the posh chap was too late.

He fell in with a terrible splash
And a scream and a shout and a roar,
He floated beneath the Transporter
Then he struck out and made for the shore.

Then somebody rescued the top hat
And handed it back to the chap,
But alas it had shrunk in the water –
And now looked just like a flat cap!

Brambles Farm Primary School

Moving Backwards

'Weeds and rust, rust and weeds! I can imagine a party of antiquarians a hundred years hence exploring the ruins of the extinct town and observing to one another that the world had not lost very much by its disappearance.' (Douglas Goldring, writing about Middlesbrough)

1
The first step is the most important
(Plato's *Republic*, see Book II)
Or you might end up where you oughtn't –
As towns like this so often do.
This lyric fountain outside mima's
A hazard for unwary dreamers,
So watch your step as we re-trace
The steps that brought us to this place.
For those who're always Moving Forward
This is a chance to learn the knack
Of turning round and walking back
The way we came, by heading shoreward
And putting History in reverse.
That is, we're going from bad to worse.

2
From bad to worse? Such condescension
Sounds rather like we're tempting fate;
These days, despite our best intentions,
Tomorrow's always out of date;
And if we think the past unpleasant,
What should we say about the present?
We need a Virgil (or Ian Stubbs)
To point out that these clubs and pubs
On Albert Road in former ages
Are where the town once kept its cash;
Now Friday nights, out on the lash,
The town comes here to spend its wages.
The banks, of course, don't think it strange,
And no-one stops to counts the change.

3
Because we do not have a TARDIS
To take us back, we'll have to walk,
And as we do, we'll try our hardest
To let the architecture talk
Above the roar of passing traffic
(It might help if you're telepathic)
Above us on the A66.
This road is like the River Styx –
On this side is the living present,
On that, the kingdom of the Dead
Whose emblem is this severed head.
On Zetland Place the Bath-like crescent
Stares vacantly, as if to say
Abandon hope, who pass this way.

4
A town is more than bricks and mortar,
We all need beauty, hope and art –
Which brings us to the Cultural Quarter,
Where web-designers get to start
What Webb & Company once finished.
With optimism undiminished
We start again. And then once more,
As though we've not been here before.
We're climbing now, to old St Hilda's,
Up Cleveland Street, towards the sky.
Here ancient buildings come to die,
Like monuments to all the builders
Whose every bright new start succeeds
The last. What lasts is rust and weeds.

5
On Tower Green we've reached the summit
Of our ambition. After this
It's all down hill. Before we plummet
Down Durham Street we almost miss
The market square once sketched by Lowry.
Graffiti tags grow wild and flowery
Like tattoos round the old Town Hall;
Although the writing's on the wall
We don't know how to read the data –
Some runic language which consists
Of dates and names in scribbled lists
(As least this gives it listed status!)
Perhaps if we could read these signs
We'd understand how urbs declines.

6
When Gladstone spoke, the world was younger,
And Hercules was just a boy.
Hard labour, enterprise and hunger –
We worship what we next destroy;
The work's now blown away like litter;
These days he's working as a fitter
Somewhere down south. Come Saturday
He's back to watch the Boro play.
The seasons pass in desperation,
Slow moving as tectonic plates.
On match-days through the turnstile gates,
We count the cost of relegation,
The levelled history of a town
That's strongest when it gets knocked down

7
We've time to catch the karaoke
Just starting at the Captain Cook.
Though not as busy (or as smoky)
As once it was, it's worth a look.
Inside, a century slowly passes
As thirsty ghosts re-fill their glasses.
Peg Powler sometimes drinks in here.
She knows all this will disappear
One day, just like the old Transporter
This bridge that links the transmundane
To re-runs of *Auf Weidersehen*.
I asked her once what life had taught her
Among the lowest of the dead.
She finished off her pint and said:

8
The first step is the most important,
So watch your step and don't tempt fate
Or you might end up where you oughtn't.
Hard labour isn't out of date.
We knew that when the world was younger.
Ambition, enterprise and hunger
Are strongest when you get knocked down;
The levelled history of this town
Is all down hill and moving forward;
And if the writing's on the wall
Like tattoos round the old Town Hall,
The signs are that we're heading shoreward
To start again, and then once more,
As though we've not been here before...

Andy Croft

La Dolce Vita

Hail, prim monster,
Vestige of our golden age.

Askance,
We view your Meccano limbs
Postmodernly,
Flexing our hardwon
(and usually imported)
irony.

One of only a dozen extant:
Accolade
And knell.

Relic of a potent past,
You traversed the decades
From splendour
To ridicule.

I hear your absurdity.
It makes me feel tender,
Protective,
That this is the best our region
Can muster
As a symbol:
Neither ancient nor modern,
Stranded in a no-man's age,
Washed up
In the Tees estuary,
Crouching ponderously
Astride the banks

As we dangle
Precariously
in a generously termed
gondola

So this must be
The Venice of the North:

That's why
The parmos are so good here.

Author Unknown

My Centenary

One hundred years, why it's hard to believe,
But here I am, still going strong above the River Tees.
1911 when I was built, doesn't seem so long ago
Yet a telling sign is that you can now check your iPad for that info.

But age is not my only defining factor,
What I've accomplished is what gives me character
I work flat out for 18 hours a day
It can be challenging at times but I'd have it no other way.

As for the people who travel on my gondola
I welcome them on, for it is always an honour.
During my career in terms of awards, I've gained quite a stack
I'm a Grade 2 Listed Building and have a Heritage Plaque.

I've got floodlights to illuminate me – what a nice thing to get.
Oh, and I've also appeared in episodes of *Auf Wiedersehen Pet*
All in all, I'm a very happy bridge and thank everyone who's helped me to stay
Please come to my centenary and party the night away!

Author Unknown